Building Positive Character

50 Tips on Empowerment, Overcoming and Success

By Joe Egan

Egan Publications Inc.
Building Positive Character
50 Tips on Empowerment, Overcoming and Success

Copyright © 2016 by Joe Egan

Published by Egan Publications, Inc.

First edition, November 2016
Second edition, January 2020

ISBN: 978-0-9851544-4-8

Dedicated to Mary, Bill, Katie, Avery and Kinley

Acknowledgments

Jennifer Havir for publishing guidance, layout and editing.
Mahieu Spaid for document submittals
Dean Korthof for great thoughts and advice.

Acknowledgements

Table of Contents

Preface

You will have character-forming experiences often. These experiences occur when something happens that creates either a good or bad experience and that experience leads to emotions. Those emotions lead to reactions, which lead to behavior, which then defines your character. When you are in a situation and you are "feeling something", can you put your finger on what it is you are feeling and why? Can you control it?

Whether the emotions are positive or negative, they must be managed through emotional intelligence, which has two elements: internal and external. Internal emotional intelligence is your ability to detect and manage your own emotions. External emotional intelligence is your ability to detect and manage your reactions to the emotions of others.

Emotional intelligence is one part of the picture, and the things we choose to dwell on in our minds is another. Predominately positive thoughts lead to positive character. Predominantly negative thoughts, on the other hand, lead to negative character.

It seems that often we reflect too long on the negatives and not enough on the positives in our lives—is it because we somehow feel guilty about being happy? This book was written to encourage you to maximize your victories and minimize your setbacks, emotionally speaking. Perhaps this can be a survival guide so when the inevitable setbacks come, you will be more ready to accept them and react through positive character.

Assertiveness

Assertiveness is best when you boldly stand your ground without stomping your feet.

Assertiveness is directly expressing your self- assured beliefs and feelings with principle, sureness and conviction. It is different than the negative nature of aggressiveness. Don't be intimidated by size, power, or authority. While you don't want to be known as a pushover, you also don't want to be "the meanest one in the valley."

Assertiveness is positive behavior and is linked to pleasure in the brain whereas aggressiveness is negative and is linked to anxiety. When confronted, use your brain, not your brawn.

Surprisingly, bullies will often back down after confronting you. Why? They are not used to being confronted and become confused as to how to react, so instead they back away from their hostile aggression.

Author Sharon Bower stated, "The basic difference between being assertive and being aggressive is how our words and behavior affects the rights and well-being of others." Assertiveness is linked to integrity and is required when the actions of others offend your values. Honesty and transparency are some of my values, so when some of my business partners tried to pull a fast one without my knowledge I decided to leave the company rather than condone their behavior. Asserting what you believe to be right allows you to be proud of yourself and respected by others.

Dr. Martin Luther King asserted his belief and principles in his "I Have a Dream" speech, but there was a cost. He spent years in jail and faced discrimination, and eventual assassination, for asserting his beliefs.

Those who are assertive are often admired—especially those who are assertive in the pursuit of justice, freedom and truth. Assertiveness is acting in your best interest and is the term that stands between your goal and its realization.

Attitude

Attitude is a matter of personal choice. It is the key that either locks success away from you or opens it up to you.

Optimism and pessimism are attitudes you are free to choose and embrace. Whether good or bad, your thoughts make you who you are and are often difficult to change. They direct your self-fulfilling prophecies. A self-fulfilling prophecy is a conscious message sent to the subconscious part of your brain—and such prophecies will produce either a good or bad outcome depending on what you have forecasted. Success is propelled by positive self-fulfilling prophecy. When you predict that things are going to go well for you, that prediction can alter your actions and cause it to come true. The same is true for negative predictions stemming from your negative attitude.

Positive or negative self-talk becomes reinforced into the paradigm that you have determined and produces evidence to support your belief. If you think you will not get the next project at work, then you are right. As President Abraham Lincoln stated, "Always bear in mind that your own resolution to succeed is more important than any one thing."

The fact that you have the ability to think also means you have the ability to control your thoughts. Your success is not certain. It is the result of attitude, so consciously send messages of success to your brain. Allow yourself to be optimistic and to expect good things. Your attitude is also expressed in your body language, which can reveal your positive or negative posture.

Positive thinking is not about fooling yourself—it is about creating yourself. A big step in this mindset is obtaining self-confidence, meaning the ability to trust yourself in the belief that you can attain your ambitions with eyes wide open about the challenges ahead. What do you get out of life? It isn't what you hope or wish for, but rather what you expect and earn. Realize that the best thing or the worst thing in your life could be your attitude.

Behavior

Behavior is guided by your decisions, not your condition.

Whenever I left home as a child my mother always said, "Now behave yourself." She never gave me a definition of the word "behavior", but I figured out I should act like her and follow her values of kindness and consideration toward others.

Behaviors can lead to goodness and health or they can lead to self-destructive paths, as in the case of addiction. But what drives your behavior? Why do you do behave like you do? When you engage in an action, you are trying to feel good. Maybe you are working extra hours so you can pay off a debt, and thus feel better about your financial situation. Or maybe you are eating ice cream as a way to cope with some emotional pain. While that may feel good momentarily, it will not benefit you in the long run.

What feels good in the short term is often not the best choice. That is why your behavior must be guided by your values as opposed to your feelings. Your values (assuming you value the right things) will lead you to make the best long-term decisions. Your behaviors are also influenced by your self-talk, whether positive or negative, and this self-talk is transformed into action.

Plants and animals also behave as a result of responding to events and environmental change. A robot's behavior is guided by computer programing. Unlike robots, you are free to choose and decide your course of action. Behavior is not about your thoughts or emotions; behavior is what you actually do. Author Stephen Covey stated, "It's not what happens to us, but our response to what happens to us that hurts us."

On the other hand, behavior is often a result of positive or negative thoughts and emotions. Your behavior over time will turn into habits, and they will lead to much of the success or lack of success in your life.

4

Body Language

Body language is what is actually being said.

We humans have been around for approximately seven million years, yet we only started to talk to each other about 250,000 years ago. Before that, we hunted and gathered food, and protected each other by the simple use of grunts and body language. Today, our body language accounts for approximately 60% of our face-to-face communication. About 30% is voice pitch, tone speed and volume. Only 10% of our communication is the spoken word.

Body language is primarily communicated through the various movements of your body and facial expressions. They honestly and perhaps unknowingly express your feelings and thoughts. Body language is therefore tied to your perceived character. When meeting someone for the first time, the other person will make an evaluation about you, right or wrong, good or bad, within the first few seconds. Depending on your body language, the other person will instantly evaluate your appearance, level of trustworthiness, level of aggression and likability, and degree of competence. Hence the saying: "You only have one chance to make a good first impression."

Give someone a firm handshake and look them in the eye to signal confidence, honesty and cooperation. When someone is tilting their head with raised eyebrows or eye squinting, they are interested in what is being said. When someone is lacking eye contact, drumming a table or picking at their clothes, they are bored with what is being said. When someone is biting their lip, looking down or scratching their head, they are confused or doubtful about what is being said.

No single body language signal should be interpreted as a correct indicator of what is being communicated. Always be aware of the body language signals you transmit to maintain a high degree of appearance, trust, calmness, likability and competence. Observe body language in others to determine if you want the other person to be your friend or simply an acquaintance.

Busyness

Procrastination-based busyness can be used to postpone the fear of failure and to protect us from accountability of results.

Although comforting, self-imposed busyness can be a diversionary port in the storm. Keep your focus on short-term, trivial urgencies in order to avoid the more important and difficult issues of long-term consequence.

When a problem needs a solution that is difficult to generate, people often stick their heads in the sand of short-term urgency and chase drama. Discomfort and distress build tension in us. We have to ask ourselves, "Do I want to focus on what is urgent, or on what is important?"

Guilt-based busyness is based on the belief that life is limited to an endless list of things do. You must realize that life should be more about things to enjoy rather than a to-do list.

Our society has high regard for those who are successful and dedicated to the pursuit of that success. But staying busy on an endless treadmill for the sake of staying busy does not guarantee success. Often being too busy can put your mind someplace other than where it should be. One of my mindless acts when I was too busy was asking my wife where my car keys were and she stated, "In your hand." Another time I left the gas station with the pump hose still connected to the car. In this last example, I paid for fast food at the pay window, then drove right past the pickup window empty-handed!

Busyness is the thief that robs you of the most important things in life such as health, family and friends. Take a well-deserved (and probably long-overdue) personal break every day, even if it is just for a short period of time. Just like in sports, take a time out and schedule time to regroup and calm down. Recognize and appreciate balance, peace, creativity, potential, options and your freedom. There is another advantage: personal breaks do not cost anything but they have big payouts.

Character

Character is exposed when you do things when other people are not looking.

Character comes from the cumulative effect of your choices over a long period of time. Good character comes from self-discipline and is rewarded over time. Bad character comes from selfishness and is punished over time. Good character is-respected by the wise and includes: trustworthiness in doing what you say you will do and the credibility of your statements, courage to do the right thing, bravery when it is needed, respect through empathy and values, responsibility through diligence in duty, fairness in justice, playing by the rules and community involvement through compassion and volunteerism. What better compliment can someone give another than to say they have good character?

Bad character is a stain upon oneself. It includes: arrogance, hot-headedness, deceit, dominance, hypocrisy and jealousy. What greater condemnation can someone receive than if someone says they have bad character? Character is at the very center of who you are.

It remains a mystery why some people choose good conduct while others choose misconduct. It seems that our minds make determinations based on education and experience whereas our character is determined by our thoughts and choices of good or bad.

Some people attempt to explain misconduct due to an unfortunate childhood, bad parents, or poor social conditions, but so many people with great character have survived tremendous struggle.

Character has no boundaries because it is exposed when things are going great or when things are going terrible. Perhaps character is formulated and strengthened through struggle, not ease.

Character is more than reputation. Reputation is what others think you are; character is about who and what you really are. President Abraham Lincoln stated, "Character is like a tree and reputation like its shadow. The shadow is what we think of it; the tree is the real thing."

Conflict

Conflicts can't always be won, so choose the ones that you can win.

Disagreements between people can often be negotiated, but conflicts must be won or lost. Conflicts are a fact of life. Engaging in them takes courage and can result in personal growth. The conflicts I refer to here are not the ones that are won or lost by physical combat, but instead by superior intellect and indisputable facts. Some conflicts can be a waste of your intellectual and monetary capital, resulting in hollow victories which are tantamount to defeat.

The joy of winning must not cloud the decision of whether to fight or just express an opinion and move onto something actually worth the effort. Some conflicts are worth the effort, especially when you are faced with something that is incompatible with laws and codes or your own principles and ethics. That is when people should fight for what is right. Unites States patriot and philosopher Thomas Paine stated, "The harder the conflict, the more glorious the triumph. What we obtain too cheap, we esteem too lightly."

In addition to conflicts between people, we each have psychic conflict within ourselves caused by the struggles between opposing needs, desires and impulses. These conflicts can be triggered by emotions and temptations. They can usually be controlled by counting to ten or by deciding if you are going to side with the angel on one shoulder or the devil on the other.

When deciding whether or not to enter into conflict ask yourself, "If I do this, how will I feel about it six months from now?" Conflict often arises out of misunderstanding or ignorance. Take into consideration there may be a difference between the real conflict and the assumed one. Be principled about choosing your conflicts. Do not choose conflict as a remedy for retaliation or antagonism. Although that may feel good in the short term, it will take you off the high road and lead you down the low road of bitterness and regret.

Courage

Courage is having the guts to face fear when you are afraid.

Courage is a requisite for the mastery of fear, danger, risk and intimidation. Courage means having the guts to face your weaknesses and the truths. The amount of courage one has determines the expansion or contraction of his or her life.

Courage is an attribute of good character and is a virtue that is held in high esteem along with justice, wisdom, prudence and temperance. It is something that everybody wants and is universally recognized as important—there's a reason for this. As poet Maya Angelou wrote, "Courage is the most important of all the virtues because without courage, you can't practice any other virtue consistently."

The opposite of courage is cowardice, which is considered a character flaw. With cowardice, fear or selfishness override what would be the right thing to do. Courage is also about trusting your intuition, standing up to evil, speaking your mind, expanding your world and dealing with personal suffering and death. Courage makes you worthy of respect, so every day that you are fearful, take action against it. Understand that fear seeks only to hold you back; step into your courage and see your life expand.

Courage starts early when your parents released you from the protective training wheels on your bicycle and allowed you to take risks. Later in life, it takes courage to jump off the high dive or ask someone out for a first date.

When I think of exceptional courage, I think about September 11, 2001, when firefighters and other rescuers ran into the burning World Trade Center towers. We saw courage on a level that the evil, inhuman attackers would be unable to conceive. The ethereal facial expressions displayed by the first responders trumped any personal trepidation over their impeding peril. I believe they entered knowing angels were by their side, and knowing for certain about their very near tragic future.

Emotional Intelligence

Emotional Intelligence is the ability to recognize and manage your emotions, as well as the emotions of others, without getting too emotional about it.

Emotional drama is about unfolding intensity and conflict. Emotional Intelligence is about containing, interpreting, measuring and managing emotions. It is closely tied to Social Intelligence and is more important in many ways than IQ, which is considered by many as too narrow of an indicator of our knowledge beyond academic achievement.

Emotional Intelligence has been around since humans evolved, but its title was not established until the end of the 20th century. Emotions do not discriminate by age, race or gender; they are equally classified into positives or negatives. I believe the top ten positive emotions that people want to experience are comfort, amazement, anticipation, pride, optimism, happiness, desire, relief, pleasure and passion. The top ten negative emotions that people want to avoid are disgust, hurt, anger, regret, pain, frustration, alienation, bitterness, contempt and rejection.

Logic stems from the left brain, which is bound by time and thinks in numbers, parts, specifications and sequences. Emotions stem from the right brain, which is not bound by time and thinks in images. It is the source of intuition, imagination and creativity. It is also the seat of conscience, gut feelings and hunches.

People with high Emotional Intelligence seem to experience a balanced life along with lower stress, greater happiness and treasured relationships. High Emotional Intelligence is linked to empathy. It is present in high performers with good social skills, mental health, leadership skills and customer service tendencies. Low Emotional Intelligence is present in low performers. Author Brent Darnell stated, "The people who excel are the ones with higher levels of

Emotional Intelligence. Not that technical ability is unimportant, but it can only take you so far."

Empathy

Empathy is life's mirror. It is the reason we smile at a smile and tear at a tear.

Empathy is having the ability and the desire to share the thoughts and emotions that someone else is experiencing. It's a trait that I believe not all people possess, but one that is required in order to understand, and therefore support another person. In building character and positive relationships, empathy is a simple matter of collecting emotional information about the other person. The more you collect, the deeper the relationship.

Empathy is a gift derived from what you have gone through in life, even if it was something bad you experienced. Difficult experiences are more likely to make someone "feel the pain" of another person going through similar experiences.

Most people have some ability to empathize with others, but I'm not sure that it can be taught. People with high empathy have the ability and motivation to understand and adopt another person's viewpoint. They share emotions when something happens that affects both parties and they desire to help others. They also don't have a problem shedding a tear over the announcement of bad news. President Theodore Roosevelt stated, "No one really cares about how much you know, until they know how much you care."

Narcissists are people who lack empathy and instead only have great interest and admiration of themselves. They have no remorse for those they have hurt and no concern for those who are hurting. They are also poor listeners who don't have a problem interrupting when someone is talking. They may try to fake having empathy but it is easy to measure their insincerity and artificiality.

Empathy lets you feel something in your body even though it really happened to someone else. It makes forging a strong bond much easier. That bond results in greater trust as you and the person you are empathizing with can share personal thoughts, worries and doubts as well as proud achievements, dreams and goals.

Evilness

An act you may know but cannot understand.

For good people, it is easy to understand about goodness because we rely upon each other for survival and positive social interaction. Evilness is hard to understand and accept because it involves selfish violence and cruelty upon another. Its motivation is for the purpose of harming others or the amusement of seeing others suffer.

The most troublesome part about evilness is that the wicked acts are intentional and lacking any morality. I think the worst form of evil is when it occurs on the basis of religious conviction. It is unreasonable and intolerable to justify religious righteousness through the act of killing people. Good people cannot empathize with or understand the reason or motivation for such acts. That lack of assimilation prevents the comprehension of the mind of the evil doers.

There is no common agreement amongst philosophers about the nature of evil. It has remained bewildered since the age of Roman philosopher Plato back in 400 BC who stated, "To do injustice is the greatest of all evils."

Good people may fantasize over the idea of committing an evil act, such as revenging your jerk boss who fired you for no good reason, but good people do not carry out the act. You don't have to go far to witness evil. Simply read a newspaper or watch the news to see constant articles and reports about war, murder, clergy child abuse and robbery.

Good must triumph over evil and it is a humane and civic duty to do so. Statesman Edmund Burke stated, "All that is necessary for the triumph of evil is that good men do nothing." Thus we have city, county, state and federal law enforcement officers and the military attempting to keep the evil people away from the good people. From evil you can learn what not to do by doing the opposite of evil, which includes being moral, helpful, trustworthy, responsible, honorable, respectful and protective of others.

Failure

Failure is most often just a temporary defeat encountered on the road to success.

$\mathbf{F}$ailure is a fact of life and becomes prominent only when you let it establish your mindset. Failure should be anticipated and you should have a predetermined reaction ready to go when it occurs. Failure is not always long-term and it provides important lessons for what not to do in the future.

The problem with failure is that it creates a tempting opportunity to just give up because that is the easy way to avoid future risk and frustration. You have to grab failure by the throat and say, "No, I will not let you win!"

People who have a strong character are not afraid of failure. They are judged not by how many times they fell down but instead about how many times they got back up. They are like a rubber ball, they get thrown down and bounce right back up.

There is a tale of Harvey Firestone, founder of Firestone Tire and Rubber Co. who discovered the vulcanization of rubber by making the mistake of spilling some on the stove where he was heating the rubber mix.

Consider the famous case of Inventor Thomas Edison and the light bulb. After thousands of failed attempts, a young reporter asked Edison if he felt like a failure and thought he should give up. Edison's reply was priceless. "Young man, why would I feel like a failure? And why would I ever give up? I now know definitively over nine thousand ways that an electric light bulb will not work. Success is almost in my grasp." A mere one thousand attempts later, Edison invented the modern light bulb.

How many failures have you suffered on the way to your success? It is strange, yet obviously true, that failure and success are mixed in the same bottle. Don't avoid a challenge just because of the risk of failure; usually failure is one step closer to success.

Forgiveness

Forgiveness is voluntary. The victim can choose to either grant or deny forgiveness to the offender.

Forgiveness is very special and personal. It is subject to many conditions, judgments, emotions and experiences. Each instance of forgiveness is unique, and the choice lies solely with the victim.

Forgiveness can be very difficult. This is especially true when you have been deeply hurt and the person who hurt you is completely unrepentant. Why should you forgive them? They don't deserve it!

The reason you forgive isn't because the other person deserves it. Forgiveness is done because it benefits the victim, the one who was wronged. Forgiveness is not condoning, excusing or pardoning the offense. Instead, forgiveness is a release from the feelings of contempt felt toward the offender. Forgiveness, according to some people, is to provide a get-out-of-jail free card called "forgive and forget." Other people don't see it as being so free, convenient and unconditional. Victims will tend to deny forgiveness when the offense comes from an intentional and malicious act of the heart, with the purpose of hurting someone. On the other hand, victims will often choose to forgive singular and temporary acts of poor judgment. That type of poor judgment happens to all of us. We are all human and that's our condition.

Denying forgiveness turns into a heavy heart filled with anger and bitterness. So instead think of it as "for-giving". "For" signifies that you are moving forward. You are "giving" yourself a lesson in life and that lesson is to not act like the offender.

Forgiveness can then be a silent thank you card. When considering forgiveness, know that time is in your favor because eventually the scars of your wounds will lessen in pain. Forgiveness removes the shackles caused by conflict, betrayal and bitterness. In the end, forgiveness is all about healing and freedom.

Freedom

Freedom is the inner peace we possess when unchained from the bondage of unjust restraint.

Freedom is not free. I have attended many military funerals for those Killed In Action (KIA). They fought and died protecting our freedom. Freedom, therefore, is a precious gift that must be honored. Freedom allows you to act without constraints with liberty and autonomy. Freedom is granted to you in many forms, such as your gift of being an American citizen, your personal freedoms and the freedom to exert leadership.

American freedom comes from the liberty and ability to be self-reliant and it should never be taken for granted. It must be honored for others and protected for yourself. Unfortunately, freedom is most treasured after it has been taken away.

Freedom is also your self-determination in choosing to react optimistically or pessimistically to any event. This was most demonstrated by POWs and how they mentally survived. Yes, there are many terrible surprises that a positive attitude can't prevent. When they happen, be in a position to exercise your freedom to respond with an attitude and perspective on top of a ladder rather than down in a ditch.

Leadership freedom is giving people autonomy to move forward, make decisions, take calculated risks, make mistakes and recover. President Ronald Reagan stated, "Freedom is one of the deepest and noblest aspirations of the human spirit."

Think about what life would be like without freedom. Without freedom you may not have the opportunity to become better, do better, express opinions, change careers or even cross state lines. Respect and cherish your freedom, but don't take advantage of it because many people have fought and died in order to protect it.

Friends

Friends are the ones who stay with you all the way; others are just acquaintances.

Friends are unconditional and earn your confidence. A friend is a lifetime gift that comes complete with a shoulder to rest on, an ear to speak into, a heart of empathy and a mind of wisdom—even after you have put your foot in your mouth. Your truest friends will bring out the best in you and you will bring out the best in them. But where does friendship start?

Psychologists have determined that when you meet someone for the first time, within the first few seconds you make assessments about them—good or bad, right or wrong. In addition to outward appearances, you observe things such as trustworthiness, level of aggression, likability and competence. Those who pass the test are best suited to transition from acquaintance to friend.

The characteristics for friends include mutual interests, shared values, interdependence, trust and emotional support. In addition, the recipe for true friendship will include the ease of geographical proximity, willing self-disclosure, reciprocal communication and mutual positivity. Another important characteristic is the willingness to give and receive constructive criticism.

With real friends you don't have to worry about the dynamics of who is in front or in charge. As the French philosopher Albert Camus wrote, "Don't walk behind me; I may not lead. Don't walk in front of me; I may not follow. Just walk beside me and be my friend."

Friendship is the reciprocal activity of supporting who the other person is while they are supporting you. Friendship is confirmed when bad things happen and you observe who stays in contact and who does not. It is unconditional, unselfish, generous, kind and thoughtful. It is the perfect example of the Golden Rule: "Do unto others as you would have them do unto you." That rule has requirements to fulfill in order for it to work. Those requirements include empathy, compassion, equality and the desire to avoid conflict.

Guarantee

None of us are guaranteed our next breath. The world owes us nothing.

Though many of us have surrounding friends and family who we think we can rely upon, there's also a sense in which we are on our own in the world and are guaranteed nothing. Even written contracts and guarantees aren't guarantees in the most proper sense as they include conditions, exceptions, exclusions and time limits—so be careful about giving them total reliance.

Hard work is not a guarantee of result, just as education is not a guarantee of wisdom. Living healthy is not a guarantee of a long life. A promise is not a guarantee of fulfillment, and belief is not a guarantee of truth. Some guarantees default due to the breach of trust.

Yet, you must proceed in life with giving it everything you have and go for broke in trying it all; don't hold back. Plan what you want to do if there is a tomorrow. Do this without assurances and security in order to maximize your undertakings and achieve success. Author Ken Poirot stated, "Take action: success is not guaranteed but inaction will guaranty failure."

Success is not guaranteed to any of us, but you can be guaranteed that you will not be successful if you don't put in the time, work, commitment and right attitude. There are no guarantees but that is part of the thrill of it. What fun would a race be if you were guaranteed victory? What fun would it be to watch a game if you already knew the outcome?

The fact that you don't know what comes next is what makes life so interesting. However, there are guarantees for failure, such as not trying, self-doubt, blaming others and giving up too soon. Just be sure you live well every day. Do your best at work and at home. Let those around you know you love them; let those you work with know that you appreciate them. Try to have your best day with your best self every day, without the expectation of guarantee.

Happiness

Happiness is one of the few gifts that you can volunteer to give to yourself.

Happiness is the most important thing to enjoy. It occurs when you choose to appreciate the exact moment you are in.
Happiness ranges from the feeling of pleasure to the absence of pain. The Dalai Lama stated, "The purpose of life is to be happy." Happiness does not always stem from money, but it does come from optimism, freedom, volunteerism, generosity, social support and eating chocolate. Most important is accepting yourself because happiness comes from within.

In America we have the right to life, liberty and the pursuit of happiness. Sad people refuse to be happy and instead decide to perpetually reside in their realm of misfortune and nothing more. They may know that happiness is a deserved right, but they feel it is somehow out of reach, so they give up.

Happy people acknowledge life's misfortunes and decide to still be happy. Happiness is beyond pleasure and fun moments. It's a fundamental drive to achieve perspective and fulfillment. It is not simply blocking the sources of displeasure because that will never end.

Thousands of psychiatrists have come up with their definitions of happiness—there is no consensus on a single definition. Perhaps it is because happiness is a subjective and emotional state of mind, and everyone has a different mind. My ten-point checklist for happiness is: (1) know it is an option; (2) maintain your positive emotions and replace negative emotions with positive ones; (3) commit to being an optimist and avoid those who prefer doomsday, negativism, pessimism, bitterness and regret; (4) anticipate that things will go bad so have a positive reaction in reserve when it does; (5) realize that any bad experience could have been worse; (6) remember you can't change the past or control the future, but you can control and appreciate your happiness right now; (7) laugh at your stupid self; (8) acknowledge the existence of good and evil; (9) be proactive more than reactive; (10) smile, love and be loved.

Honesty

Honesty is external truth-telling and the internal willingness to recognize your strengths and weaknesses.

Honesty leads to trust and respect, and therefore the ability to influence people. A high form of honesty is the ability to communicate constructive criticism with decency and directness. Honesty is easy when things are going great, but challenging when things are terrible. Truthfulness is honesty that is sometimes difficult to say or hear, but not as hard as unwinding from a lie.

To be effective and respected, you must act with honesty and integrity. This means acting in such a manner that people will trust you to handle any matter in their best interest.

Internal honesty requires the willingness to recognize your strengths and weaknesses. Doing this gives you the ability to maximize those strengths and minimize your weaknesses. Honesty is the basis and prerequisite for the ability to successfully manage relationships.

Honesty is both a discipline and a choice. It can be a tough choice, just as Humorist Kin Hubbard stated, "Honesty pays, but it doesn't seem to pay enough for some people." Truth cannot be hidden for long. There will be times when marginalizing the truth will ease the issue for a time. But you must be true to yourself; you must be bound by the truth, which is not the easy course.

Dishonesty is tied to hypocrisy, greed and unfairness, which leads to a lonely life lacking both friendships and a good reputation. Narcissists are the champions of dishonesty to both themselves and others. They are the heroes of the fairytale they live in as they hide behind a cloak of values and ethics that they preach but don't practice. Lying is part of their playbook so they can present false images of themselves in order to impress or deceive someone. Some narcissists lie just for the fun of it.

Honesty truly is the best policy—if you can't be true to yourself, what is your reason for being?

Hope

Hope is the daydream that gets you from one circumstance to the next.

Hope is its own opposite. Internal hope is what you hold in your heart. It allows you to believe that possibilities exist and can give you confidence and motivation to achieve a future expectation. However, external hope thrust upon you by others just might be selling you a promise that can't be fulfilled. Such false external hope is sometimes used by politicians when selling an empty promise in order to get your vote. Those falsehoods, when revealed, transform hope into despair and the feeling of foolishness for believing they would fulfill their empty promise. Therefore, don't always believe what you hear, even if it is what you want to hear.

Be optimistic and rely on hope to show your potential, but also realize that hope itself is not a reliable strategic plan. Hope is about dreams and wishes and is limited to the "wanting" and not the "making" of something to happen. In your personal and business life you can't just rely upon the hope of wanting something to happen. Instead you must make something happen through realistic goals and tactics to achieve them.

A plan without hope and conviction has no vital energy to propel it forward. Likewise, hope in the absence of a plan is simply potential energy that needs to be harnessed. Hope is necessary for a plan to move forward, but it is not enough on its own.

Medical researcher Jonas Salk invented the first polio vaccine and helped rid the world of a virulent disease. He relied upon positive internal hope and stated, "Hope lies in dreams, in imagination and in the courage of those who dare to make dreams into reality."

So, embrace internal positive hope but go beyond dreams and wishes. Instead use hope as your engine for motivation and anticipation. Then take the next steps for planning, execution and fulfillment; that's what the great ones do.

Humor

Humor is what gets us through the menaces of life.

Humor is seriously important because you have to learn to laugh at yourself. The odd thing about humor is that it is different than being funny. Telling a joke or being silly is funny. Humor is the ability to let things go and not take life so seriously. It's about grinning, letting out a deep breath and saying "oh well" after a letdown.

Humor puts you at ease, allowing you to sidetrack pain. It seems odd to laugh off pain, but humor is a required tool in your survival kit. Sometimes we can't bear all the heavy weight that life throws on us, and humor can lighten the load.

Just like sight, smell and touch, you also have your sense of humor. Humor can also be used to deflect awkward social interactions by playing into your weaknesses. This simply requires that you criticize yourself in a laughing manner before someone else does so in a serious manner. Author Mark Twain stated, "Humor is the great thing, the saving thing. The minute it crops up our resentments and irritations slip away and a sunny spirit takes their place."

Humor is also a sign that you have a good grasp on life regardless of your condition. My brother Jim died young from cancer. While in hospice he used humor to deflect his physical and emotional pain. He had the instinct and conviction to take pain playfully. He refused to be a tragic person even though cancer was such an event. Humor was his defense mechanism and an affirmation of his dignity. Without humor, life could become unbearable.

Humor is also laughing at yourself. The other day while in a parking lot I failed to apply the brakes soon enough and hit a sign post that created a small dent in my bumper. Instead of getting upset about my stupidity and cost of repair I decided to smile at myself

36

and said, "That was really stupid!" Humor recognizes that you can't change what happens, but you can control your attitude about what did happen.

Intuition

Intuition is following the directions given by your inner voice.

Intuition goes by many names: gut feeling, hunch and sixth sense. It's the ever-present knowledge of what to do without the ability to prove it. Intuition is the ability to know about things that you have not seen or heard. One of the definitions of intuition is tied to clairvoyance, a French term that means "clear vision".

Though intangible, intuition is not magic. The sense of intuition is a mental state, and just as real as real as your physical senses. Some people consider intuition more powerful than intelligence. Using your intuition is both a gift and a discipline because it requires you to allow your innate senses to trump empirical observations and rational justifications.

Physicist Albert Einstein stated, "The rational mind is a faithful servant and the intuitive mind is a sacred gift. We have created a society that honors the servant and has forgotten the gift." Think of intuition as having a wise personal coach present inside you. Tapping into your intuition works best when you have a rested mind and have rid yourself of negative emotions.

Women have a larger area of the brain dedicated to intuition. Researchers suggest this may be how a mother can hear the cry of a baby too young to speak and determine if the cry is a result of hunger, pain or a need for attention. This is where we get the phrase "women's intuition".

Intuition has a way of cutting through the clutter when making decisions. There may be many pros and cons, and many tangled emotions when trying to make a difficult decision. Often your intuition will speak the truth. It is, after all, the sum of your experience, your knowledge and your wisdom speaking to you.

Apple founder and visionary Steve Jobs stated, "Have the courage to follow your heart and intuition. They somehow already know what you truly want to become. Everything else is secondary." Your intuition is worthy of your respect. Listen to it.

Leadership

Leadership has many definitions, but they all boil down to the requirement of having <u>willing</u> followers.

Leadership cannot be faked or granted; it is earned and based on the ability to inspire. It means you are in front and have people who want to and are willing to follow you. Most anyone can demonstrate leadership. It does not require being a certain age, having a specific type or length of education, having a lofty title attached to your name or being the best at working on a computer.

In fact, many of the great leaders dropped out of higher education. Being a manager, boss, director or supervisor also does not necessarily equate to being a good leader. In fact, many employees have witnessed senior managers who are terrible leaders, instead they are dictators!

Leaders achieve success by surrounding themselves with competent managers who are motivated and optimistic, and who are often smarter than them. Such leaders identify their company's values by determining what would be in the best interests of their employees and customers. Honesty, open communication, respect and continuous learning are a few of the characteristics leaders possess. In doing so, the leaders gain what is in their best interest— namely, a good reputation, loyalty and a healthy compensation plan.

Leadership also happens when one person helps others achieve their goals. Leaders of an organization become successful not through self-promotion, but through the assessment and conclusion of the followers. Leaders do not rely on domination and intimidation for people to follow them.

Leaders also understand the difference between urgency and importance. Urgency is handling the day-to-day problems that have to be solved right now! Importance is about thinking ahead and making strategic plans in order to stay in business. Leaders are responsible for concentrating on the important things while delegating the urgent things to those most capable to handle them.

Learning

Learning is the first step to wisdom.

All of us have blind spots in our lives; areas where we don't know as much as we would like. Learning is a challenge that allows you to reduce ambiguity. It is for the curious who want to transform knowledge into wisdom. Learning is like a ladder because each time you learn, you go a step higher. Learning is not compulsory—you are not required to get on the ladder. If you choose not to learn, at least understand that not learning equates to much ignorance.

Learning is more than just relying upon non-transforming instincts based upon past experiences. It is about changing your behavior as a result of new experiences. Another good reason to continue learning is to give yourself a lesson in how much you do not know. The more you know, the more you realize how much you do not know. Historian Daniel Boorstin stated, "The greatest obstacle to discovering the shape of the earth, the continents and the oceans was not ignorance, but the illusion of knowledge." There are many interpretations about what Daniel was stating. I believe he meant that if someone believes the *illusion* they know something, they will not seek to *discover* more knowledge even though they may be misinformed about their illusionary belief. For example, years ago we had the false illusions that the world was flat, the sun revolved around the earth, we only use 10% of our brain and that bats were blind.

We are all born ignorant, but through discovery, imagination and creativity you excel through the process of education, which gives you knowledge and then experience, which gives you wisdom.

You must also learn to live with what you were born with and live in the moment so you can enjoy happiness. You must learn to hold onto the good things and let go of certain other things, such as

42

the people that pester you. Finally, you must learn from a very large
impact on our lives … failure.

Listening

Hearing is not the same as listening.

Hearing is simply the vibration of your eardrum. Listening is acknowledging what is being said through your ability to correctly receive and interpret what is being said. If not correct, it results in confusion and misunderstandings. Talking is when you speak about only what you know. Listening is the opportunity to learn more or to enjoy something unfamiliar to you.

Jurist Oliver Wendell Holmes stated, "It is the providence of knowledge to speak and it's the privilege of wisdom to listen." A reward for that wisdom is found in the story about a sales person who had a 20-minute conversation with a customer. During the entire meeting the customer did all the talking while the salesperson remained completely silent and listened. After 20 minutes the customer shook the salesperson's hand and said, "Congratulations, I want to buy your product." In amazement the salesperson responded, "Thanks, but why, what did I do to deserve this?" The customer responded, "Because this is one of the best conversations I have ever had!"

Listening is more than an act; it is a discipline, especially in a society where everyone wants to get in the last word. The discipline is your ability to turn off your response mode and give a mindful and undisrupted listen to the other person. Resist the habitual temptation to jump in when the speaker pauses. This requires the discipline of concentration, patience and determination. This becomes easier through self-awareness.

Be aware that when actively listening you face the speaker head to head, looking at them straight in the eye and with your feet pointing at them. Your entire posture should be open and comforting. Being aware of such body language allows you to realize that you are practicing the discipline of active listening. Active listening does not mean that you agree with them but it does indicate that you acknowledge and respect them.

Love

Love is universally unique.

Love is everywhere and yet has a different definition for what it means, how it starts, how it maintains and how it dies. The proof of differing definitions lies in the fact that a Goggle internet search for the word "love" results in almost 20 billion hits.

Hollywood gives many ideas about what love is, and for the most part, those ideas are wrong. Contrary to the prevailing opinion at the moment, we are intended to be a monogamous species. Life just works better that way.

Love does not follow logic but it does run the entire field of emotions. Actor Woody Allen stated, "The heart wants what it wants. There's no logic to these things. You meet someone and you fall in love and that's that."

All relationships feel good at the beginning—that's a large part of the reason you enter into them. That special guy or girl looks great, is fun to be with, and makes you feel good about yourself. Naturally you want to spend more time with them. This is called "falling in love".

Staying in love … that's another story. To stay in love requires commitment as well as emotional connection. It's about volunteering to put the other person's wants and needs ahead of your own.

To build something lasting requires commitment. Families require commitment. Marriages require commitment. The best love stories are the ones told over decades and they inevitably have their share of good times and bad, abundance and want, joy and pain. These are the narratives you can find beautiful because they explain the best parts of being human—rising above faults and pettiness and reaching out to another in love over the course of a lifetime.

There is another benefit to love. If you know how to truly love, you probably do not know how to hate. If you want to determine who you truly love, think about who you would want to be with in the final moments before your death.

Luck

Luck can be both a fate and a fluke.

Making your own luck (fate) is about creating your own destiny through intuition and foresight rather than relying on the artificial circumstances of a fluke. Fluke is reserved for the good luck of winning the lottery or the bad luck of a lightning strike. Creating luck is more about discovering fortunate things by plan. It is seeing possibilities that others may overlook.

Long ago in 50 AD, Seneca stated, "Luck is what happens when preparation meets opportunity." Making your own luck sometimes requires stepping away from your secure position in life. The preparation part of making your luck is having a "ready, set, go" frame of mind that is already inclined to accept risk and failure.

Opportunity is simply a situation that provides a possibility to do something, but if it is ignored, it goes away. Therefore, opportunity requires timeliness because doing nothing is a guarantee of going nowhere. Those people who lack preparation and timing are self-proclaimed as "unlucky".

Making your own luck can even be achieved in times of difficulty, but it requires a positive state of mind. As Sir Winston Churchill stated, "A pessimist sees difficulty in every opportunity; an optimist sees the opportunity in every difficulty."

Optimists know where they are going in life and take advantage of the opportunities to get them there, all the while knowing there will be random ups and downs (the other kind of luck). They see opportunity as intriguing and recognize the potential benefits. They feel deserving of luck and are willing to go ahead without being 100% certain. Unlucky people, on the other hand, feel undeserving and instead of opportunity they see danger. They are unwilling to go ahead unless they are 100% certain.

Making your own luck boils down to realizing the power and influence of where you direct your attention and the resulting choices you make. It's the difference between could have and should have; between did and didn't.

Mind Rest

Mind rest is intentionally shutting down the self-talk without feeling guilty about the endless list of things you have to do.

Years ago the Little River Band wrote the song "Lady". The first verse states:

> *Look around you, look up here.*
> *Take time to make time, make time to be there.*
> *Look around, be a part.*
> *Feel for the winter, but don't have a cold heart.*

These lyrics teach the importance of intentionally taking time out. They tell you to empathize with people affected by harsh events, but not to let them drag your heart down. So yes, take time to make time and make that time to be there just for you—and don't feel guilty about it.

When you take time for yourself, let yourself appreciate the exact moment you are in. Don't think about what you are supposed to do fifteen minutes from now, or a day or a week later. Don't act like children who get in the car on a trip and soon say, "Are we there yet?"

Instead think about where you are right now as your destination. Yes, it's important to be responsible and plan for your future, but you don't have to be planning every minute. That way you can pay attention to what you have to appreciate in this present moment, instead of focusing on what you hope for in the future. Thinking in the moment relieves anxiety because you are not agonizing over the past or worrying about the future.

Unless you've had a super day at work, I believe it is best to leave your job out of your home. Why drag a bad day into your home when it can be left outside and ready for pick up the next morning? The amount of time between leaving work and getting home is a good time to transition from *work* mode to *home* mode.

Remember what is important to you—friends, family, home—so leave the job behind. You can pick it all up again in the morning and realize that nothing changed overnight.

Mistakes

Mistakes are the acts that humans are good at, such as using the bumper instead of the brake to stop.

Mistakes have other names. They are called errors, faults and stupidity. Mistakes also go by the names experience, wisdom and betterment. Although undesirable, mistakes provide more value than doing nothing. Pick yourself back up after making a mistake and don't agonize because that is holding onto something you can't afford to keep.

It can also means allowing people to take calculated risks and make mistakes. This is an important function in the learning curve. Yes, it is risky, but those who have been taught by their supposed leaders through consistent public and private reprimands about their mistakes eventually learn not to take any more chances, regardless of the probability for greater success. To protect themselves from further wrath, they hunker down and become afraid of being assertive. They lose esteem and confidence, and are hesitant to raise issues or offer strong opinions.

The frequently reprimanded person offers multiple suggestions and asks other people to choose which is best. They become more comfortable being a "yes person" by making suggestions as a member of a committee rather than making independent decisions based on their judgments. The result of a criticism-based culture is extreme loss of morale and organizational inefficiency in decision making, actions and results. Passion can be destroyed where mistakes are not allowed.

A healthy environment allows for taking risk and accompanying mistakes. An even *healthier* environment allows for the public omission of making a mistake as part of the culture without reprimand. That is why the wise policy at Honda Motors is, "Mistakes will not be criticized, only the concealment of them."

Rather than dwelling and loathing on a mistake that will lower your self-confidence and empower negative emotions, consider it as something valuable that you can learn from and motivate you to move forward.

Multitasking

Multitasking is mentally unhealthy and should not be a self-adorned badge of honor.

Multitasking can hurt more than help because your brain was not built for it. Your brain functions best when you focus on and analyze singular tasks. So think "hyper focus," not "multitask".

Yes, you are able to do two things at once. The problem is that you can't effectively or efficiently concentrate on two things at once. Activity does not equal results, and being busy is not the same as being productive. In fact, performing 2 one-minute separate activities takes longer than 2 minutes if they are performed at the same time.

Multitasking has many drawbacks. A key one is the lack of tact often demonstrated by multitaskers attempting to perform multiple tasks simultaneously with the goal of impressing another person with their talents in dealing with complexity. For example, it is tactless to converse with someone while at the same time talking on your phone, going over reading material, scrolling through your electronic device or flipping through files.

Instead of impressing someone, multitaskers can come across as a violation of basic relational skills. It places the other person in third or fourth place for your attention where they should be first. Author Joanne Tombrakos stated, "Multi-tasking is great in the kitchen when you are trying to time the chicken to be ready at the same time as the potatoes. But do not assume it is a great way to manage a workday."

In addition to being rude, multitasking can also make you appear inept because your brain is not designed to effectively handle multiple mental tasks at the same time. When you attempt to multitask, the available brainpower for each task is actually reduced. Serious multitaskers can experience reduced concentration and memory due to the adrenaline rushes from the mental stress required to multitask.

Narcissism

Narcissism is falling in love with the person in the mirror.

The word "narcissist" originates from the Greek legend of Narcissus, who fell in love with his reflection in the water. Narcissists are arrogant and preoccupied with fantasies of unlimited brilliance and power. They survive on admiration, attention and affirmation. Behind their cloak of confidence and superiority is a fragile self-esteem and ego. They feed on narcissist supply, which is the nourishment of their subservient enablers who support them with compliant adoration for their agenda. In return for the enablers' slavery, they get "nice" pats on the back, invited into the inner circle and allowed to keep their jobs.

Narcissists become notorious against those who do not participate in the feeding of narcissist supply and are willing to harm those non-participants. Those who do not feed are considered nonfunctioning.

Narcissists are unwilling, and therefore unable, to establish genuine relationships. They are indifferent to the problems of others and uninterested in recognizing their feelings. They spend much time in the mirror absorbing esteem, admiration and affirmation instead of releasing sensitivity, sympathy and understanding.

Their lack of empathy causes them to feel no remorse after harming or offending someone. When confronted, they lash out with disdain, rage and defiance, which can be both verbal and physical. They wish to be feared and prefer fight over flight. Even a simple question or request for clarification can be received as a personal attack.

There is debate whether narcissism is caused by internal nature or external nurture. Regardless, narcissists are selfish social morons who do not have the right to impose their personal plague onto others.

If you have to deal with them, realize they are con artists, so don't try to change them. Observe their red flags, keep your distance so you don't fall prey and be ready to pack your bags.

Negotiation

Negotiation is about getting most of what you need by giving up some of what you want.

There are as many resolutions to a problem as there are people working toward a resolution. You can negotiate, arbitrate, mediate or litigate. The easiest and most productive method is to negotiate.

Negotiating requires each party to give something up to the other in order to get their own needs satisfied. Make a list of what you are willing to give away in order to get what you want, but don't give anything away unless you get something in return.

The ability to negotiate with someone requires an open and honest rapport so that problems can be settled objectively, and without drama, for a win-win situation. This way of approaching conflict is based on the knowledge that problems will occur. With your associate, you both presume that you are going to get through each problem as it arises and prepare for the next one.

When negotiating, it is always good to bear in mind the wise words of First Lady Eleanor Roosevelt, "Never allow a person to tell you no, who doesn't have the power to say yes."

Negotiation is best when you are willing to count to 10 before hitting send. It is also best when you restrain from knocking the hinges off the door when you slam it in the other person's face.

Arbitration, mediation and litigation are the result of failed negotiations. They typically stem from hurt feelings, hard-headed egos, stubbornness and unwillingness to admit weakness. Those methods are time consuming and require expensive payments to a third party to convince you of your weakness, liabilities and vulnerabilities.

Litigation should be short for "scorched earth." Litigation happens when you draw a line in the sand with a permanent marker. Your wounded ego, distressed heart and inflamed emotions trump logic and reason. This win/lose stance is filled with negative emotions and can be motivation for retaliation.

Past

The past is what keeps coming to the present in an attempt to affect our future.

The past is perplexing and lies in the mind of the beholder. For example, several people could observe a particular event, yet all have different memories of it. If the past exists only in our memories, and our memories are subjective, then the past is subjective and the future is uncertain. They do not rise to the level of tangibility, so the only thing that is "real" is the present.

On the other hand, past experiences—both positive and negative — form our platforms for thoughts, judgments and decision-making. Rigid bureaucracies are formed when the past is used as the only platform. This results in the "well that's what we do and that's how we do it because that's the way we've always done it" mindset. This mindset doesn't serve anyone well because it sacrifices flexibility.

This, of course, doesn't mean you need to throw away your past experiences and completely reinvent yourself. You ought to learn from the past and let it influence your future plans but not completely determine them.

You are-moving into a future world; not the world that has passed, no matter how nostalgic you may feel for it. As former USA President Lyndon Johnson said, "We can draw lessons from the past, but we cannot live in it."

Living in the past and repeating bitter memories guarantees a disappointing future. Escaping the negative past requires the discipline of knowing you are in a rut and moving on from it. You can, however, mine the past for memories. Bad memories provide safeguards for what not to do in the future. Conversely, good memories provide joy, comfort and an optimistic viewpoint for the future.

The past should be about a place you depart and not a place you dwell. Unless you are living through a past tragedy, don't be consumed with the wringing of hands. Instead, acknowledge that history is history, what is done is done and let bygones be bygones.

Perseverance

Perseverance is your quiet inner voice at the end of the day that says: "I will try this again tomorrow."

Perseverance is one of the most consistent characteristics of someone who is successful. It is the willingness to reach into the dark with the will to win despite difficulty, uncertainty, delay, opposition and the risk of failure.

Giving up is easy, so instead go forward and persevere without fear. Learn from mistakes so you hopefully don't repeat them, knowing you will have the opportunity to make new mistakes when you stop dwelling on the old ones.

Don't worry about what you cannot control in the future. Adapt the behavior of steadfastness and live in your positive, imaginary future. Decisions come from values, but conditions come from feelings. Remember that behavior is a function of your decisions, not your conditions. If you choose to behave according to your feelings rather than your values, you will be reactive. Reactive people have less self-control and are able to empower the weakness in other people to control them.

Perseverance is very powerful because it upstages difficulty, setbacks, discouragement and rejection. Sir Winston Churchill stated, "Never, never, never give in."

On the other hand, there comes a time when you realize that current efforts will not result in reaching your future goal. Perhaps those goals were beyond your best abilities or even impossible to achieve by anyone. Terminating such efforts is not to be considered a failure or a "give in" surrender. It is purely an objective abandonment of an unreachable pursuit through an acknowledgement of reality.

Think of perseverance as your personal coach who inspires you to become your best despite obstacles, setbacks, pain, failure and lack of confidence. At least you tried, which is more successful than not trying at all.

Playfulness

It is fun to have fun!

Adult playfulness is tied to good character. Being unpredictable and impulsive may seem to be a character flaw in adulthood, but when tied to playfulness, it results in energetic happiness.

This type of playfulness includes the playing of sports, but also the simple humoristic acts of laughing or joking in order to put a smile on your face and the face of others.

Play and work appear to be opposite, but they are not. Work is tied to a requirement whereas play is tied to a reward for hard work. On the other hand, for a child, play is the act of working to discover their surroundings and interact with people.

Of course as we grow to adulthood we should become more serious, but continuing to play should not be viewed as petty or unproductive. It is just as important for adults as it is for children. Adult playfulness can be purposeless and a diversion, but it is not an abandonment of our serious side. You can still be a serious adult focusing on your practical purposes in life, such as strategic planning, problem solving and efficiency, while taking a healthy, temporary and spontaneous break to amuse yourself and others.

The benefits of playfulness include reduced stress, fun to be around, creativity, wit and good-naturedness. A University of Illinois playfulness expert stated, "People who are playful don't run away from stress, they deal with it - they don't do avoidance."

Playfulness should not be a personality trait by always acting like a clown. Clowning around can be construed as obnoxious, or dangerous silliness or idiotic behavior. This type of behavior will make others fear rather than appreciate your presence.

Play is a form of freedom and an escape from reality because it is self-chosen. In addition, you can create the rules and quit anytime you want. Playing is living in the moment and proceeds through life from children at playgrounds, to teenagers playing sports and to adults playing cards. It is more than a pastime, and is as important to health as sleeping and eating.

The Present

The present is a genuine gift.

Yes, it is important to reflect on the past and contemplate the future. However, it is physically impossible to live in the past or in the future. Conceptually living in the past could often be holding onto something that you can't afford to keep. Living in the future could often be trying to obtain something you can't afford to have. Living in the present is the only way you can appreciate the exact moment you are in. Living in the present is also the only way you can experience and manage your emotions and whether you choose good or bad outcomes. The present is where you decide to activate the positive feeling of optimism, happiness and thankfulness or your choices for pessimism, anger and regret.

Living in the present can also free us from distraction. How many times have you left one room in your house to get something from another room and forget why you entered that room? It is because while you were going to that room you distracted yourself by thinking about the many things on you never ending to-do list. It is difficult to live in the present because we may feel we are being inattentive to our to-do list.

You need to give yourself a break from the past and future every day without feeling selfish and simply concentrate on what you are doing right now. Even if to live in the present is simply feeling the sun on your face, watching waves on a lake, listening to nature or holding a baby. Calmly depart from your over-filled world while acknowledging and accepting your emotional state and physical being.

Use the present to create fond memories and realize everything you are thankful for. The present can provide peace of mind, creativity and certainty, whereas the future provides uncertainty. We hear children on a destination road trip saying "Are we there yet?"

The response to yourself should be *I am in the present and therefore already at my destination.*

Problem Solvers

Problem solvers are paid a premium price because they turn negative situations into positive solutions.

Problem solvers look for answers, not errors. Reporting problems is a good form of honesty and courage, but that is not enough. Problem solving requires the reporting of a problem along with the proposal of a solution.

Almost invariably those who need a problem solved will buy into your solution rather than developing one. If you can control the solution, you can control the problem. Problem solvers enjoy family respect and job security. Why? Because others rely on them to make their lives easier.

Problem solvers have the discipline and staying power to navigate the problems inherent in life. Problems can represent both challenges and opportunities. Problem solving is a personal investment with the payout being subconscious reliance from others. That subconscious reliance tells the person who has the problem that there will be resolution if they call upon the problem solver. For that reason, you ought to see being called upon to solve a problem as a compliment rather than a burden.

For employees, problem solving creates extreme customer loyalty that exceeds the company logo and enhances a résumé. I recall a project manager who complained to me in frustration about his inability to get things done on his checklist. I asked what was stopping him. He replied that customers kept getting in his way because they were calling and wanting him to solve their problems. He seemed surprised when I told him that receiving those calls is a compliment to him and said he was elevated to a problem solver, which should be his top priority. I asked him, "If all the problems were solved by someone else, what would be the importance of your job?" After this enlightening conversation, this project manager approached problem solving as a passion and position of honor rather than an irritating intrusion.

Promptness

Promptness is responding to someone before they feel offended that you are ignoring them.

Years ago some people could excuse a failed return call because of either not finding a phone booth or not having a quarter to pay for the call. Today there are no excuses because with electronic communication, you can't hide. The sender of information knows the communication was sent and the receiver knows it as well. Prompt returns are viewed by the sender as a sign of respect as well as a confirmation that the sender is a high priority and is significant to the receiver. It also demonstrates a commitment to the relationship.

When replies to the sender are ignored or delayed, things can go bad very quickly. People have a tendency to think the worst. It's similar to the worry reaction that parents have when their children are late and do not call. For parents, the worry stems from the duty to protect the child. Customers worry about their worth or value to you. An ignored or delayed reply can have the sender thinking a number of things: "What's wrong, why am I not getting a reply?"; "If I was respected I would have received a reply by now"; "There must be something much more important and a higher priority than me"; or "I feel like I'm being left out in the cold." Poet William Shakespeare stated, "Better three hours too soon than a minute too late."

Failure to promptly return phone calls, emails or text messages is an ever-increasing cause of frustration. It can transform a fragile self-esteem into a hardened heart because it is viewed as rude and disrespectful. With a continued pattern of abuse, the frustration evolves into feelings of contempt and dismissal. Likewise, a delayed response—or worse yet, no response at all—is an essential act in the destruction of relationships. It separates the respected from the disrespected, the timely from the ill-timed and the mannered from

70

the ill-mannered. There is little or no justification for a lack of response in this day of lightning speed communication.

Purpose

Purpose is what motivates you to get out of bed.

Life's purpose is not so much about your career or personal life, but the energy you carry in life. It is the reason why we do or create something and requires intention to initiate and determination to carry through. Purpose is your life's dream, drive, aim, mark and destination.

Purpose could be as easy as recognizing your unique gifts and sharing them with others. The ability to find your purpose could be as easy as asking yourself the positive questions: "Why am I here?"; "What touches me the most?"; "What gets me most energized?"; "Who do I want to help?"; or "What do I want to be remembered for when I die?".

First, you have to acquaint yourself to yourself and then create a personal mission and value-statement such as:

I will live my life based on principle and sharing my gifts with others with honor, dignity and respect. I will choose optimism over pessimism. I will not allow others to bully me and will protect those who need my help.

Many conclude that life is meaningless and has no purpose, but they are wrong. Everyone has a purpose because everyone has some experiences, talents, thoughts and desires that could benefit themselves and others.

Tragically, some people choose evilness as their purpose. They prey upon others with malicious vengefulness, ill will and spitefulness. The only good thing about evil is that it eventually destroys itself.

Just like happiness, purpose is discovered from within ourselves, and having a purpose will result in great happiness. Your purpose can't be forced because it is a discovery. Author Mark Twain stated, "The two most important days in life are the day you were born and the day you discover why." Your purpose can be whatever you choose.

Resiliency

Resiliency is the ability to turn yourself into a rubber ball. It's the power to upturn after a downturn.

Resiliency is a requisite and universal trait of triumphant people. Whereas perseverance is the steady ability to go forward in a course of action, resiliency is the ability to bounce back after unfortunate events. It's about realizing that difficulty and misfortune are facts of life coupled with the ability and motivation to rise from the ashes.

Resiliency applies to both mental and physical health, such as recovering from an injurious accident or depression. It also applies to recovering from a financial loss.

Pick a difficult goal—anything you really want to achieve in life. Because your task is not easy, it will take time. You are going to have trials and setbacks along the way. You will have to begin each day with a goal in mind and keep moving toward it despite the inevitable obstacles. Reaching your goal will require flexibility, the will to recover and strong belief in yourself.

Years ago I was involved in a construction project that lost three million dollars. Soon after, I decided to quit and change my career to something not as difficult. I had then said to myself, "This is an opportunity to see if I can pick myself back up and be stronger for surviving the struggle." I decided to remain-in my position with the company. Even though I lost all my hair and had stomach ulcers from the stress, I did not lose my resiliency and I was able to bounce back.

Giving up is always an option and will free you from the burden of trying harder. Before giving up consider the quote from author Charles Classman, "If you're planning on quitting, first make sure it's not for one of these reasons: fear, discomfort, anger, self-pity, someone's negative opinions, past failures or unrealistic expectations." Like a battered but undefeated boxer, perseverance gets you back in the ring after being punched out.

Respect

Respect is not granted; it's an earned distinction.

Respect for self is having the conviction to not tolerate the intolerable. Respect for others is having the conviction to grant recognition and dignity to those who deserve it. It is important to have self-respect, but it can be just as important to give it. Respect is tied to esteem whereby you may have high self-esteem or have high esteem for those with who you associate.

Respect is also tied to honor and dignity, yet it is different. Honor is behaving unselfishly toward others and having the inner power available to give tribute to others. Honor is bestowed because of what you give, not what you receive. Dignity is having decorum and being generous while taking your rightful place in the world. Dignity cannot be taken away unless it is surrendered.

Political leader Nelson Mandela stated, "For to be free is not merely to cast off one's chains, but to live in a way that respects and enhances the freedom of others." Respect is an attitude and is contrasted with reverence, which is an emotion. Respect is bestowed out of principle, not out of fear. Respect is a method of living for yourself while giving deference to others, especially to those who have served and are serving in the United States military. Respected people are considerate, obliging, good listeners and don't finger point or make excuses.

People will often respond to the degree of respect you have for them. If you lack respect for a person or group, this can turn into a self-fulfilling prophecy. You will act in a negative manner and carry the attitude to justify your predicted outcome. If you believe a person hasn't earned your respect, you will treat them accordingly, and your thinking will likely be confirmed.

On the other hand, if you believe a person is worthy of your respect, then you will treat them accordingly and your thinking will once again be confirmed. One prophecy is doomed for failure and the other prophecy is destined for success.

Self - Talk

What we say to others matters, but what we say to ourselves matters the most.

How many times when you are alone do you find yourself engaged in self-talk? No, you are not crazy, and we do flood ourselves with self-talk with approximately 50,000 thoughts per day. That in turn educates our subconscious to carry out the self-talk. Those thoughts and resultant orders from our conscience brain do not care or judge if the self- talk orders are positive, negative, right or wrong. It will simply fulfill the message received and thus impact how you feel about yourself, others and life in general.

Self-talk is natural and will be healthy if you keep it positive. Positive self–talk includes statements such as: "I know this is going to be a great day."; "I'm good at my job."; "I'm very thankful for my health." Negative self-talk includes: "I look terrible in these clothes."; "I'm so stupid."; or "I will never get another job."

Self-talk must be balanced and judged with reality. Excessive positive self–talk could be detrimental by being overly optimistic about unrealistic goals. Ignoring negative self-talk could be detrimental as well if we ignore activities and people who could harm us. Author Gino Norris stated, "Your self-talk is the channel of behavior change."

There are many things in life that we can't control, but we do have total control over our self-talk. If your self-talk is nonstop chatter, then take it upon yourself to slow it down. You may then find you have more energy at the end of the day by not being mentally exhausted. If you self–talk is primarily negative, then stop beating yourself up and proceed upon the challenge of changing from a pessimist to an optimist.

After all, it is your mind so you should be able to control what it says to you. A great tool to assist your mind in self-talk is self-confidence by assuring your opinions and ability to succeed. Another tool is self-trust, which is the steadfast and optimistic refusal to give up on yourself.

Smarts

Smarts is the ability to recognize, blend and summarize information in order to make proper judgments.

W ebster's dictionary defines smart as "showing intelligence or good judgment... mentally alert...shrewd." In this case, shrewd is the closest to what I mean. We all know people that we would call shrewd. What common traits do they have? Some people equate shrewdness to a rude and selfish character. On the other hand, shrewd people are very well informed, energetic, witty and clever. They go beyond "book smart", which is equated to knowledge, and instead are "street smart", which is related to experience and wisdom. It is thinking from intuition instead of from a manual.

You can't be shrewd without the relevant information. Sometimes the people with the highest IQs are not the shrewdest people. If someone is intelligent (maybe they have a PhD in biology) and they know nothing about the stock market, they can hardly be expected to make shrewd investing decisions. Author Matshona Dhliwayo stated, "The smartest fish are still in the sea."

Shrewd decision making means seeing through all the clutter and the noise. They make patterns out of facts, then separate fact from fiction to determine a good direction. Shrewd people are often financially successful, but typically only spend money on necessities.

They also ask a lot of questions, listen more than they talk, and have secrets they don't give away. Shrewd people may have charisma, but do not want to be the center of the crowd. They listen to their gut, are quick on their feet and use common sense to then take action.

The opposite of shrewd is defined as "naïve". Not to say that being naïve is negative or weak, it is simply being unexperienced and unwise. This could easily be justified due to someone's background, young age, experience, education, or level of trustworthiness.

Smile

A smile is the most important thing you can wear.

A smile is an ornament of peace and an adornment on your heart. It is a sure sign that you have a good handle on life and it makes you more likable and approachable. A smile is one of the few expressions that are universal throughout the world and are constant regardless of age, culture, race or religion. Smiles are understood by everyone and display a wide variety of communication including happiness, love and even embarrassment.

Smile even when you are not happy because it fools your brain into thinking you are happy. This may sound silly, but can a simple smile really change anything? Even if the mechanism isn't clear, it's clear that smiling does have a powerful effect.

A thirty-year longitudinal study by UC Berkley looked at students' yearbook photos and how they were smiling. By examining their photos, the study could predict how fulfilling their relationships would be and how inspiring they would be to others.

When you genuinely smile, the outside of the eye shows slight crow's feet, the lower eyelids tighten up, nostrils are slightly flared and the outer lips of the mouth face upward. A fake smile is displayed in the form of a grimace, which is an expression of disapproval or anxiety in attempt at comic exaggeration. The expression of the grimace shows squinted eyes, wrinkled nose and twisted lips.

A smile can be used as a tool both internally and externally. Internally you can physically place a smile on your face. Try this when you are alone while counting your blessings. Immediately your mental state will improve and stress will reduce. Externally use the smile as a tool to solicit a smile back. Try this when walking down the sidewalk—give a stranger eye contact with a smile. Unless that person is very distressed, you will immediately receive a smile back.

So smile often and without reason. You'll add health to your body, years to your life and brighten up the room around you.

Social Interaction

The more you are connected, the more you may become isolated.

There is a growing and concerning social activity whereby the more you are connected to your electronic device, the more you may become isolated from face to face interactions.

This is not meant to be a criticism but rather an observation of reality. However, what becomes lost through the isolation is the all-important exchange of emotions, which cannot be relied upon as being accurate through electronic communication. Often these virtual interactions are miscommunicated because the receiver has a different interpretation of what mood was in the sender's mind when the communication was sent.

For example, let's say you texted someone about a recent accomplishment that you worked hard for and are proud to share with others. You then receive a reply simply stating "Really!!" That one word response could be interpreted in many ways both positive and negative such as "Oh really? I doubt you actually did it!" or "Really, that is great, I am proud of you."

Another loss is the important aspects of meeting someone for the first time. If that meeting is through electronic messaging, you lose the ability of determining the important and accurate first impressions. You also miss out on body language and tone of voice which also reveals personality and character. Author Alex Morritt stated, "The more time we spend interconnected via a myriad of devices, the less time we have left to develop true friendships in the real world."

Lack of face to face interaction can be embarrassing as an employee or acquaintance. How would you feel if you only texted someone who lives in your town for years and then went to visit and say, "When did you change your hair style?" with an answer of, "About a year ago."

Success

Success is not the accumulation of material things, but rather the measure of the value you bring to yourself and others.

Success is most often achieved through the persistent will to manage and reverse the hardships of failure. Expect to trip on failure while on the path to success, and also triumph in your personal victories. It is not selfish; it verifies the reason to become better.

Many people who have accumulated large amounts of monetary wealth are considered successful. Likewise, there are many wealthy people who are failures in many ways. Yes, you need money for the basics in life, but beyond that money plays a minor role in the equation for success. The accomplishment of wealth, celebrity and power can lead to satisfaction, but is susceptible to short-lived duration and an unquenchable thirst for more.

Success depends on the accumulation of non-monetary factors that don't matter where you live or what type of family or job you have. The ten factors I include are: (1) persistency in achieving goals; (2) respect and empathy in treating people; (3) high expectations of oneself and others; (4) the ability to negotiate for a win-win rather than a win-lose; (5) unconventional, positive and progressive thinking; (6) humanitarian efforts; (7) realizing strengths and weaknesses; (8) choosing optimism over pessimism; (9) getting from the problem to the solution; and perhaps most importantly, (10) successful people are trusting and trusted.

You can be financially successful by being untrustworthy, but that is not what defines success. Instead, being untrustworthy is one of the main prerequisites for being a failure.

Businessman Arnold Glasgow stated, "Success is simple. Do what is right, the right way, at the right time." Doing right carries the responsibility of bringing others up with you, so give others your helping hand. Begin where you are at, employ your tools and perform the best you can.

Talent

Talent is an endowed gift not to be ignored or flouted.

Talent is unique because it is unspecified from birth, yet it is manifested by innate ability. The seed of talent remains a mystery. It does not appear to lie only in our genes. If that were the case, the children of Bach, Stravinsky, and Mozart would all be great music composers.

Talent is both physical (sports, art and acting) and mental (empathy, sixth sense and composing). Talent is different than genius. Talent is what you have; genius is what you know.

Are you talented? Yes, I believe that everybody is talented because talent is a natural ability to do something even if it is not being taught. Talent is a gift; like any other gift, the best response is to be grateful. You should be thankful for that natural endowment.

It's important to recognize that talent is only a starting point. For talent to serve you well, you must master it through the realization of your potential; otherwise it is just a waste. Author Madeleine L' Engle stated, "We can't take any credit for our talents, it's how we use them that counts."

If you do manage to harness your talent and are successful, be willing to bring others up with you. Remind them that talent alone never has been, and never will be, enough. You must overcome the fear of failure and harness your talent with hard work. President Calvin Coolidge stated, "Nothing is more common than unsuccessful men with talent."

The thing about talent is that if you don't use it you may lose it, and that would be a huge waste of potential. Talent gives you the unique capacity to achieve and succeed.

Unfortunately, many people with great talent—such as some professional athletes—allow their talent to go to their heads and selfishly equate their gift with supremacy and privilege over others.

Respected talent requires the thankfulness of aptitude and the humble appreciation of your gifts.

Trust

Trust is a one-on-one activity that allows the other person to be in a position to take advantage of your vulnerabilities while you are expecting they will not.

T rust is extremely fragile and can be forever broken when the wrong thing is said at the wrong time for the wrong reason. Trust engaged is perpetual, while trust betrayed vanishes.

Trust is the gateway to successful relationships. It is the ability to predict what other people will do and what situations will occur even if you do not know all the facts. Trust is feeling safe with another person when managing the expectations, roles and goals of your promises.

When commitments are not met, the caustic emotion of betrayal may take over because one's freely offered vulnerability has been taken advantage of. The intangible becomes tangible in a way that includes disgust and bitterness.

For someone to trust in you, they are supposing that at some future date your promises will be kept. They stand naked in the hope that you will not betray their trust and take advantage of them. Trust and lack of trust are found at a delicate crossroad, each having significant implications. As Director Frank Crane stated, "You may be deceived if you trust too much, but you will live in torment if you do not trust enough."

People have keen internal safeguard monitors that can identify untrustworthiness immediately. Researchers have concluded that trustworthiness (or lack of it) can be determined within seconds through body language and intuition. Those monitors can detect evasive answers, lack of eye contact and suspicious body language.

The best way to support your pursuit of a trusting relationship is to give it time. Earned trust is the result of having a series of interactions in which the other person perceives that they are being treated fairly and treated well.

Values

Values are our perceived rules for what we believe is worthy.

Successful people value trustworthiness, dependability, loyalty and sincerity. There are hundreds of values and are unique to each person. Your personal values dictate why and how you behave as well as the priority you give things. Your values are your principles and the basic tenets that you are willing to stand for.

I have not met anyone who is willing to die to protect their material accumulations, but I do know people who have been willing to die to defend and protect their values and principles. Those are the people who place great worth on protecting their families from harm and their country from its enemies. They do this on their own terms and within their hearts because they embrace family and freedom as their highest values. Spanish philosopher Jose Ortega stated, "Tell me what you pay attention to and I will tell you who you are."

Values that are considered most important include: kindness, honesty, co-operation, love, respect and trust. Values are included in the transformation of feelings, judgements and conduct. It is similar to character because it demonstrates either the confirmation or the contradiction between what you say and what you do.

A person with no morals is "Amoral". They do not have an understanding or concern of right or wrong. They are unprincipled without standards or scruples, and are often spontaneous and dangerous because they act without restraint.

Values are about your willingness to uphold your high ethics and morals, and to respect someone as much as you respect yourself. Honesty and transparency are some of my values. When some of my business partners tried to pull a fast one without my knowledge, I decided to leave the company rather than condone their behavior based on my values of being principled and honest. My values allowed me to take action consistent with what I knew what was right and wrong.

Volunteerism

The ability to enhance the quality of life in yourself and others.

In my younger years I did not volunteer because I believed that activity was reserved for older people who had nothing else to do. Later in life, I did not volunteer because I had very limited available time. Along came my opportunity and need to volunteer. An important and trusted person in my life betrayed me and left me feeling bitter and in situations where I was uncomfortable meeting and engaging with new people. I knew I had to snap out of that negativity and discovered the affirming, trusting and constructive aspects of volunteering. Being with other volunteers demonstrated the esteemed values of compassion, empathy, honor, dignity and respect.

The world is full of fierce competition and pursuit of materialism, which I consider as "cultural" nature. Also in the world are unselfish acts, including laying down one's life for the benefit of others, and I consider as "human" nature.

The most significant act of volunteerism that I am personally aware of was demonstrated by two construction workers who I met shortly after the bridge they were working on collapsed into a river. They told me that instead of running for their lives to shore they remained on the wreckage pulling people out of cars who were about to drown. I asked them, "Did you fear for your lives?" They responded, "No, we were too busy helping people!"

In addition to saving lives, volunteering provides the feelings of purpose and happiness. The purpose is to make a positive impact upon others and happiness derived from that purpose. Medically speaking, helping others increases your brain's pleasure hormone called Dopamine. It is your brains neurotransmitter that drives your brain's reward system and feeling of well-being. Comedy writer

Robert Orben stated, "Here's to all volunteers, those dedicated people who believe in all the work and no pay."

Worry

Worry is a colossal waste of time and energy because it cannot affect the outcome of what you are worrying about.

Worry is an optional emotion about real or imagined issues. It is different than caution. Caution is an act, such as strapping your seatbelt, wearing a helmet or avoiding lightning. You can worry if the plane will be on time; if it is going to rain on your outdoor party; or the thousand other "what ifs" in life, but it produces nothing but anxiety.

Try not to let yourself be tormented by the fear, anxiety and burden of worry. Worry is something that wants to get into your head, but you don't have to let it even though it is a natural part of life.

Worry not only affects your emotions, it can also cause physical problems including restlessness, headaches, ulcers and tense muscles. It is can also be a gateway to substance abuse.

When dealing with worry, realize that you don't have the ability to script your life but you do have the ability to script your thoughts and reactions. Just because the pilot says there will be turbulence does not mean the plane is going to crash. This is not foolishness in thinking nothing bad will ever happen. Instead, it is a disciplined tool for better mental and physical health.

A funny way to realize the futility of worry comes from this quote by Peanuts creator Charles Schulz, "Don't worry about the world coming to an end today. It's already tomorrow in Australia."

On the other hand and depending on the severity of a potential negative or dangerous situation, "Don't worry, be happy" could be irresponsible and foolish. Think of it as, "don't worry, be neutral." Suspend the worry until the facts arrive. Meanwhile, contemplate what your reactions will be when the facts do arrive.

So the next time you are poised to worry, think of the Serenity Prayer, "Grant me the serenity to accept the things I cannot change; courage to change the things I can; and the wisdom to know the difference."

Conclusion

Thank you for reading this book. I hope it made a positive impact on your future thoughts, actions and reactions to all the positive and negative encounters you witness every day. Always keep in mind that predominately positive thoughts lead to positive character. An example of this is that thoughts of confidence transform to assertive character. The same thought-to-character transformation is also true for courage, listening empathy, tolerance, forgiveness, honesty integrity, resiliency, perseverance, expectation and trust.

Predominantly negative thoughts, on the other hand, lead to negative character. When conflict elevates to betrayal it can result in a bitter character, one that is too suspicious to ever trust someone again.

It seems that often we reflect too long on the negatives and not enough on the positives in our lives—is it because we somehow feel guilty about being happy? Do not feel that guilt because we are culturally free and mentally obligated to the pursuit of happiness.

I recall more than once that people have attempted to criticize me by saying, "Why are you always so happy?" The answer is because I use my freedom to choose to be an optimist instead of a pessimist. That way when difficult things happen in life I am mentally prepared to ask myself, "How am I going to react? What am I going to do?"

Think of the positive *yes* instead of the negative *no*. *Yes* advances opportunity and *no* ignores it. *Yes* starts communication and *no* stifles it. *Yes* encourages action and *no* prohibits it. *Yes* leads to collaboration and *no* leads to isolation. *Yes* leads to discovery and *no* leads to suppression.

Have your best Y*es* D*ay, every day!

Joe Egan

About the Author

Joe started in construction at the age of 14 where he was working as an apprentice and remained in the industry for 45 years. He held senior management and ownership positions at several large construction companies. Those years provided great successes and failures. He has made and lost millions of dollars and experienced the joy of trusting relationships and the devastation of betrayal.

He has lived a unique life that provided the motivation and credibility to author this book which demonstrates the vital importance of building positive character through the ability empower yourself to embrace the good things and to overcome the bad things in life, all of which leads to personal and business success.

To live in harmony with the good and bad in life you need to make good choices, by finding your purpose, prioritizing values, using common sense and the pursuit of happiness.

Joe believes your personality comprises distinctive groups of emotional traits. It is who you are. Character is what you do with yourself. Character is about morals and ethics; it's what you do even when no one is looking.

Combining personality and character is to join thinking and doing. This book combines the "thinking personality" with "character's doing" to help you successfully navigate everyday events, emotions and reactions.

Joe's philosophy on building positive character is based on building a respected reputation based on integrity and follow through. It also includes focusing on the objective mission, not the dramatic moment while embracing problem solving as a positive opportunity for improvement.

www.ingramcontent.com/pod-product-compliance
Lightning Source LLC
Chambersburg PA
CBHW031600040426
42452CB00006B/368